RHYTHM GUITAR PLAYING

BOOK TWO

GW00655946

GRADE 3 — GRADE 4 — GRADE 5

BY

CHAZ HART

A CIP record for this publication is available from the British Library

Published in Great Britain by

RPL
REGISTRY PUBLICATIONS LTD

Registry Mews, 11 to 13 Wilton Rd, Bexhill, Sussex, TN40 1HY

Printed and bound in Great Britain

v.20130211

FOREWORD

Registry Of Guitar Tutors (RGT), in association with London College Of Music Exams, first began to offer grade examinations in electric guitar playing in 1993. Since that time the examinations have proved to be highly popular with students and teachers alike. However, the RGT has repeatedly had requests for additional course material to accompany the *Rhythm Guitar Playing* section of the examinations. This series of three books by **Chaz Hart**, an ex-RGT electric guitar examiner, has been especially designed to fulfil that need.

Each book provides a wide range of musical examples that clearly demonstrate the type of chord progressions that will appear in each grade of the examinations. In addition, Chaz has thoughtfully provided *Playing Tips* with each piece. These give advice on the most common problematic areas and offer suggestions on how to gain those extra elusive marks. Because of Chaz's wide experience as a teacher and examiner, these comments are always insightful and poignant.

Overall the series provides a structured and progressive way of approaching the study of rhythm guitar playing and will undoubtedly provide a valuable study method for all students of guitar – whether intending to take the examination or not. In addition, the series serves as an excellent teaching resource which guitar teachers can use to complement their teaching programme.

Tony Skinner

Tony Skinner
Director – Registry of Guitar Tutors
www.RGT.org

RHYTHM GUITAR PLAYING
BOOK 2

From my experience as a teacher and electric guitar examiner, I've found that one of the main difficulties facing guitar players, is not having enough chord charts to practise in a full range of keys. This book aims to alleviate that difficulty. All of the chord charts have been officially approved by The **Registry of Guitar Tutors** for use in their electric guitar examinations, which are organised in association with **London College of Music Exams**. The book is written in a progressive manner, so that even if you are planning to take the Grade Five examination it will be helpful if you work through ALL sections of the book from Grade Three upwards.

You'll find that I've made many references in the Tips section to using each piece as a test, and not stopping, but it's the one thing in any musical situation that you must not do, so... I make no apologies for saying yet again – DON'T STOP.

There are a few progressions that will come up many times, and if you know these it will help you play through them with ease. Below are some of the most common changes, which I have written in the key of C, but practise them in every key:
The numbers represent the positions in the scale of each chord, and will be the same in EVERY key.

I	VI	IV	V
C	Am	F	G

I	II	V	I
C	Dm	G	C

I	III	VI	V
C	Em	Am	G

If you work out that C (5th string root) is on the third fret, the **IV** chord (F) is always two frets lower (6th string root), the **V** chord (6th string root G chord) is on the same fret as the C chord, and the **VI** chord (6th string root A minor chord) is two frets higher. These changes will be the same in every key.

Good luck,

Chaz Hart L.R.A.M.

Introduction

Note values The following notes and their names are shown together with their basic comparative values:

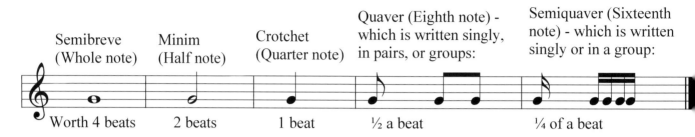

| Semibreve (Whole note) | Minim (Half note) | Crotchet (Quarter note) | Quaver (Eighth note) - which is written singly, in pairs, or groups: | Semiquaver (Sixteenth note) - which is written singly or in a group: |

Worth 4 beats   2 beats   1 beat   ½ a beat   ¼ of a beat

Rests The following signs are rests which last for the same amount of time as their note counterpart, but as silence...

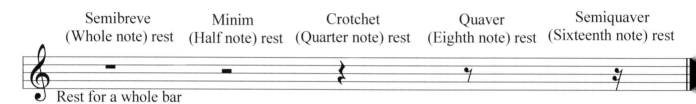

Semibreve (Whole note) rest   Minim (Half note) rest   Crotchet (Quarter note) rest   Quaver (Eighth note) rest   Semiquaver (Sixteenth note) rest

Rest for a whole bar

Time signature

This is the number that appears after the treble clef sign at the beginning of a piece of music. The top number indicates how many beats to count in each bar, whilst the number underneath shows the value of each beat. In this grade you need to know the following time signatures and these are shown together with the most commonly used strums. Notice how the quavers (eighth notes) in a $\frac{6}{8}$ time are counted as the main beat because the underneath figure is an 8 (which denotes a quaver value) - however the first of every three beats is accented, giving a feel of 'two in the bar'.

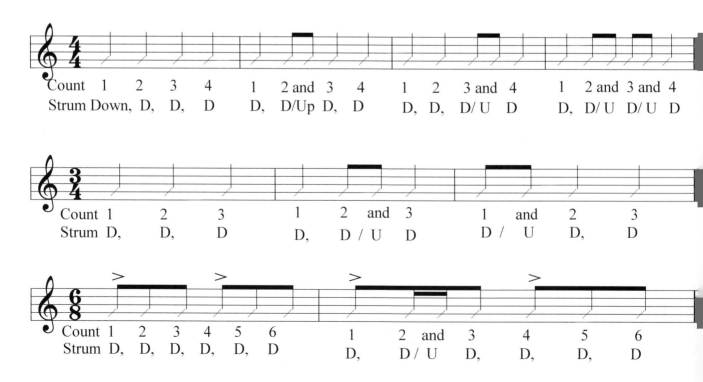

Grade Three

There are four different barre chord shapes to learn for this grade. Whilst the barre chord shapes can be learnt fairly quickly, the trick is to learn the notes on the 6th and 5th strings up to the 12th fret, this will then give you all the chords you need for this grade. (See page 32 for chord shapes).

Repeat Marks

Sections to be played again are marked with two vertical dots at the start and end of the bars. The only exception to this is when you repeat from the beginning where the start dots are omitted. This sequence would read: | C | G | F | G | F | C |

1st & 2nd time endings

The bar marked with a **1.** is played the first time, and then omitted and replaced by the bars with **2.** the second time. Hence the sequence would read: | A | D | A | E | A |

Split bars

These bars contain 2 chords. Each split bar chord has a dot after it which indicates another beat. In $\frac{6}{8}$ time each chord has 2 dots after it to show the other 2 quaver beats, but the bar is still split equally at this grade.

Dynamics

These indicate changes in volume and the signs and their meaning are shown in the next sequence - which is easier than usual so you can practise one thing at a time!

5

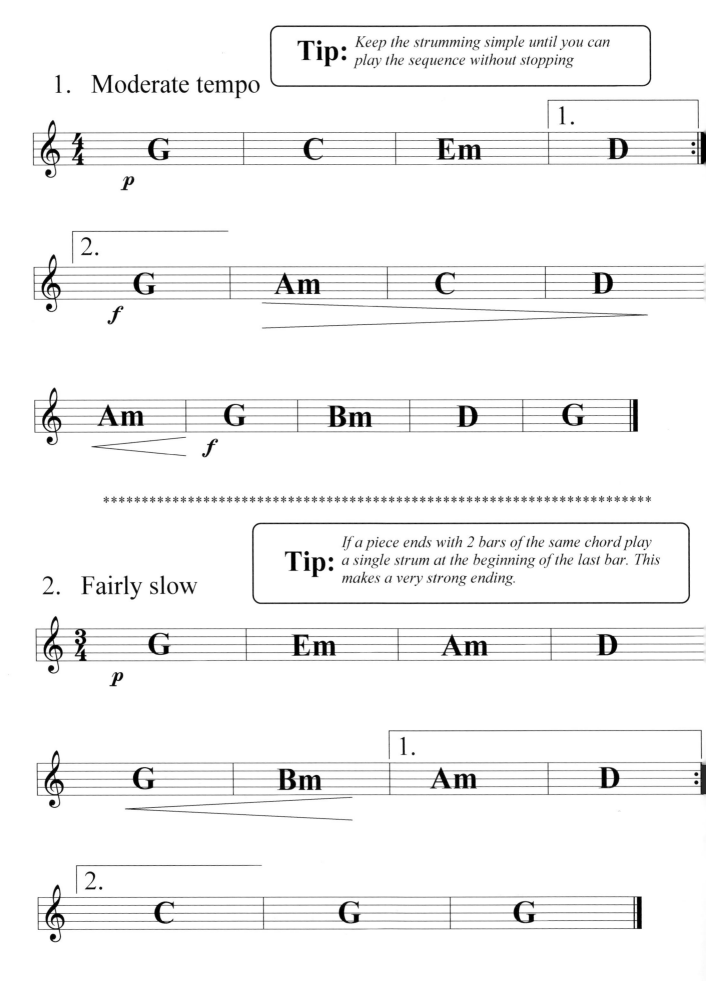

Tip: *Use these sequences as a test. Take your time looking at them to assess YOUR best tempo.*

3. With a rock feel

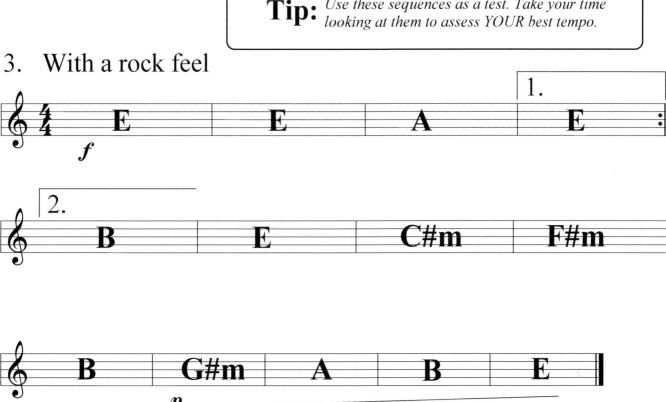

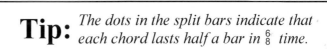

****

Tip: *The dots in the split bars indicate that each chord lasts half a bar in $\frac{6}{8}$ time.*

4. Slowly

> **Tip:** *Keep your fretting-hand wrist and elbow relaxed. This will help you move from chord to chord freely.*

5. With a beat

****

> **Tip:** *Although the tempo indication is 'fast', be careful not to overplay this and make errors in the split bars.*

6. Fast

Tip: *Watch out for the split bars and the short repeat sections between the double dots.*

7. With a blues feel

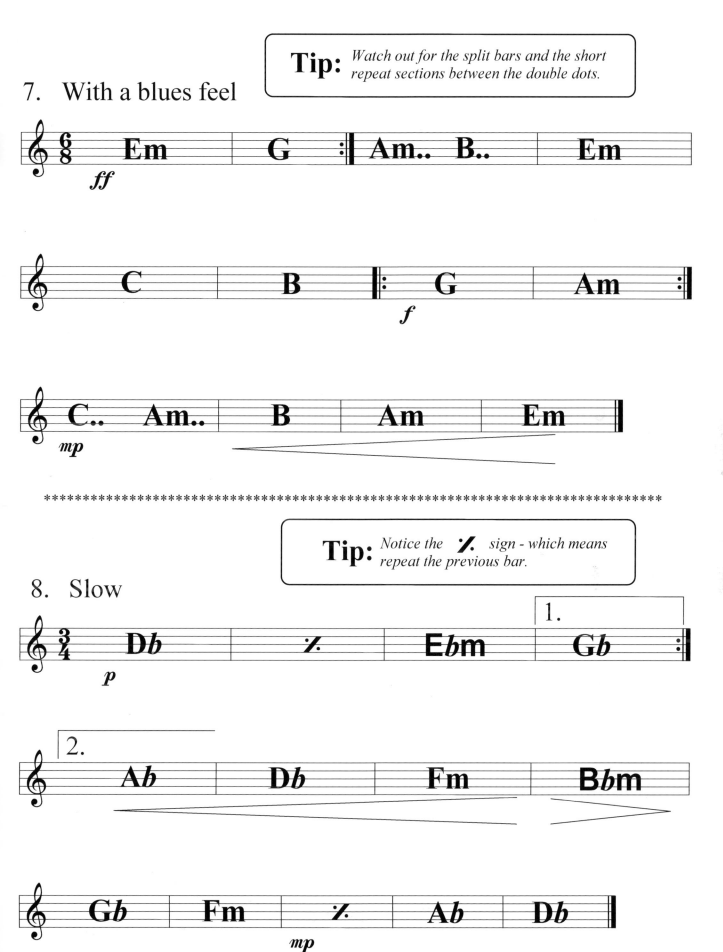

Tip: *Notice the ⁒ sign - which means repeat the previous bar.*

8. Slow

9. Uptempo

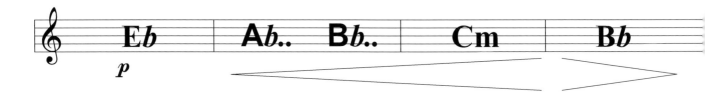

****

10. With a swing feel

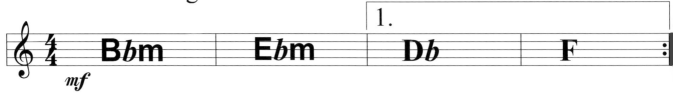

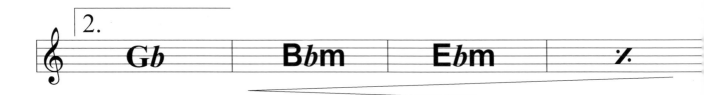

Grade Four

Repeat marks In this grade the repeat marks are the same as for Grade Three, so please refer to page Five.

Tie notes This is where two notes of the same pitch are shown with a curved line joining them. This indicates that the second note of the pair should not be played, but held on. The numbers in brackets show a note counted but not played. For example:

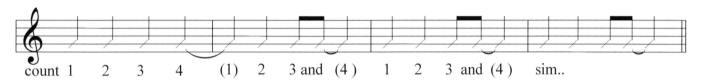

count 1   2   3   4   (1)   2   3 and (4)   1   2   3 and (4)   sim..

Syncopation This is commonly known as accenting the 'off' beat, and is one of the best ways to modernise a rhythm part. Notice how the last note in bar 1 seems to come in early in bar 2. This is known as a 'Push'. Be careful to wait for the whole of the first beat in bar 2, otherwise the tempo could increase. The rhythm pattern in bars 3 and 4 could be played over *Wonderful Tonight* by Eric Clapton.

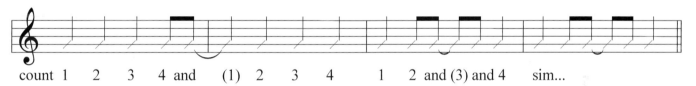

count 1   2   3   4 and   (1) 2   3   4   1   2 and (3) and 4   sim...

Syncopation The key to successful rhythm playing is to move your hand down on the main beat even when you're not striking the strings on that strum, as with these syncopated timings, so that your hand is ready to play the 'Up' strum in the correct position. Practise this until it feels right and I assure you that your rhythm playing will dramatically improve. Here are two more lines of rhythms for you to practise. The first line rhythm could be played over *Roll With It* by Oasis.

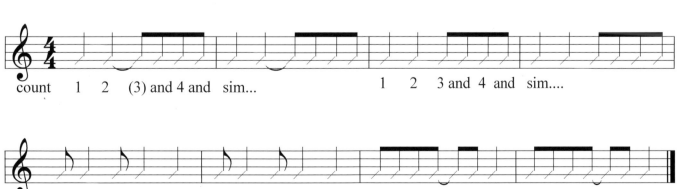

count   1   2   (3) and 4 and sim...   1   2   3 and 4 and sim....

1 and(2) and 3   4   sim.....   1 and 2 and (3)and 4   sim....

Variations in strumming

O.K., now we have explored the syncopated route, let's put it into practice. Below are three well known strums in the three time signatures that you need for this grade. Practise them on your favourite sequences until you can't play them wrong!

> Note : In the Registry of Guitar Tutors examinations the rhythm patterns that you play will NOT be notated, so it's up to you to have practised a repertoire of useful rhythm patterns from which you can select an appropriate one for the style of the piece.

count   1   2   3 and (4) and   sim.....

1   and   (2)   3   sim......

1   2   3   4   5 and 6   sim.....

Dynamics

These signs are broadly the same as in Grade Three, but with more range. It would be a very strange piece that used all of them in one section, so I have written out the new ones for this grade together with their meanings. Notice how they are varying degrees of soft to loud.
Go on – Give that E chord a really good whack!

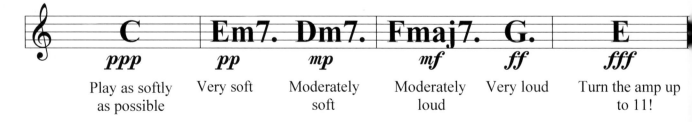

C	Em7. Dm7.	Fmaj7. G.	E
ppp	*pp* *mp*	*mf* *ff*	*fff*
Play as softly as possible	Very soft Moderately soft	Moderately loud Very loud	Turn the amp up to 11!

1. Lively

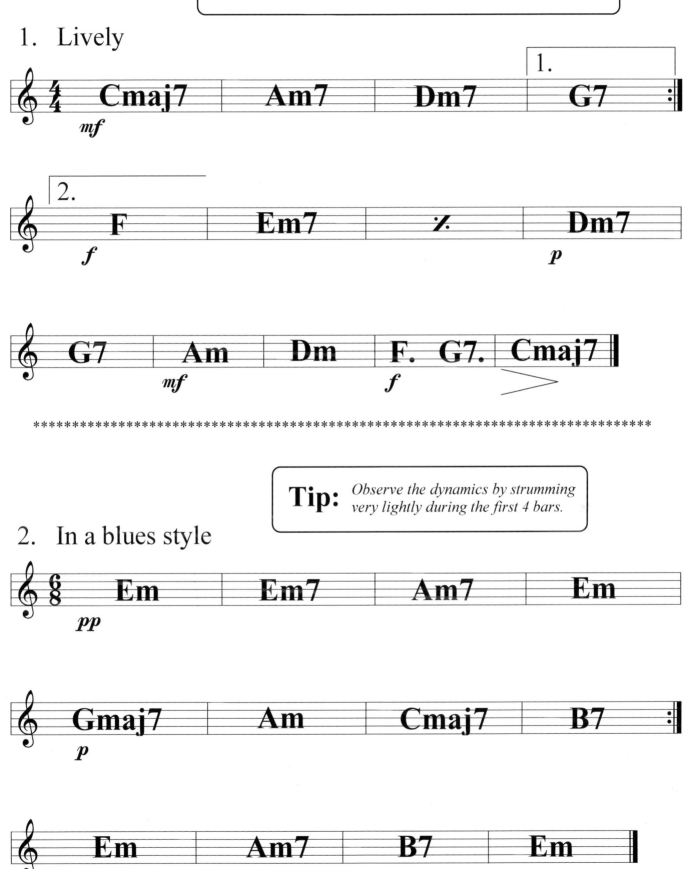

2. In a blues style

3. Moderate tempo

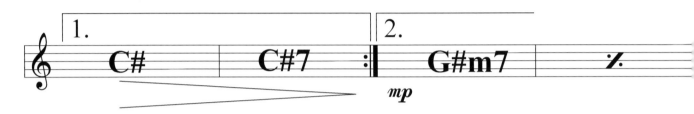

****

4. Slowly

14

5. Waltz tempo

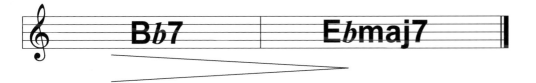

****

6. Slowly

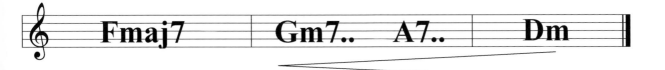

7. In a blues style

****

8. Freely

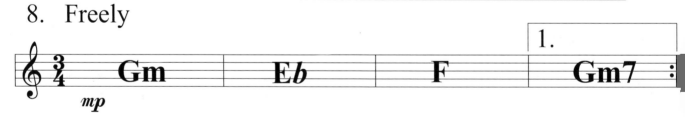

9. Bright & lively

****

10. Slow with feeling

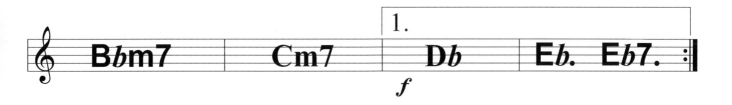

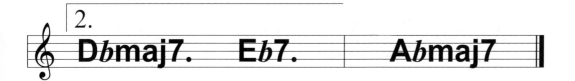

Grade Five

Repeat marks

The repeat double dots and first/second time endings are the same as for Grade Three and Four, so please look back to page five for an update. However, there are some new repeat signs for this grade:

D.C.	-	Play again from the beginning
D.S.	-	Play again from the sign 𝄋
Al Coda	-	Go to the ***Coda*** from the sign ⊕ after a section repeating from a ***D.C. al Coda*** or ***D.S. al Coda***
Coda	-	A musical end section

Here are some examples to play through:

1.

This sequence would read: | E | E | A | B | E | E | A | B |

2.

This sequence would read: | C | F | G | Am | C | F | G | C |

3.

This sequence would read: | D | G | Bm | Em | F#m | Bm | Em | A7 | D |

Split bars

We have seen in previous grades that a bar can be split between two chords, and that these can be written in the following ways:

Or in $\frac{6}{8}$ time showing the two dots for the quaver beats:

The bar could also be split into different parts, or with more chords. The most common sequences are where the bar has three chords with the first chord having two beats and the latter two chords one beat each:

In $\frac{3}{4}$ time, with only three beats in a bar, one of the chords could last two beats with the other chord lasting one beat.

Rhythm Patterns

The time signatures for this grade are still $\frac{3}{4}$ $\frac{4}{4}$, and $\frac{6}{8}$, so I feel that you should be thinking of varying the rhythm on the repeats as a necessity rather than a luxury!
I have written the first two bars of the following three sequences straight, followed by bars three and four as a variation, usually with some syncopation. In practice you would possibly start with the rhythm that featured less detail and go to the fuller rhythm as the piece progressed.

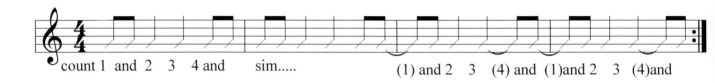

count 1 and 2 3 4 and sim..... (1) and 2 3 (4) and (1)and 2 3 (4)and

count 1 2 3 and sim..... 1 2 and (3) and sim.....

count 1 2 and 3 4 5 6 sim.... 1 2 and (3)and 4 5 6 sim.....

Dynamics

These are the same as for Grade Four so please look back to pages five and twelve, and practise them over many sequences.

1. Bright & rhythmic

2. With a beat, but not too fast

E.   G#m7 Gm7 | F#m7 :‖ A.   C#m7 Cm7

mf

To Coda ⊕

Bm7 | A.   B7. | Emaj7 | C#m7

f   *p*

F#m6 | G#m7 | Amaj7 | E

f

D.C. al Coda

F#m | Bsus4 | B7

⊕ *Coda*

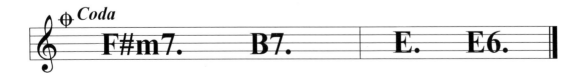

F#m7.   B7. | E.   E6. ‖

22

> **Tip:** *Watch out for all the repeat sections. This sequence looks short but has the same number of bars as the previous piece.*

3. In a ballad style

Cm7 | ∕ | Fm7 | ∕ | E♭maj7

p

To Coda ⊕

F7 | Cm | A♭maj7

mf

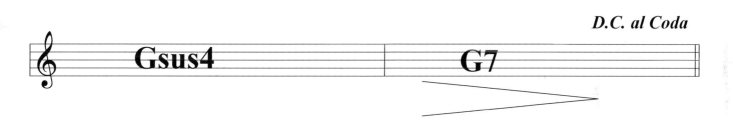

D.C. al Coda

Gsus4 | G7

⊕ *Coda*

‖: A♭maj7 | B♭ | G7 | Cm7 :‖

f

4. With feeling

To Coda ⊕

Dm   C   B♭   A7

mf

Dm7   Fmaj7   Gm   A7

f

D.C. al Coda

Dm   C   Gm7   Gm

⊕ *Coda*

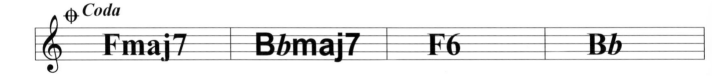

Fmaj7   B♭maj7   F6   B♭

Asus4   A7   Dm

p

> **Tip:** 1 - *An effective way to play a split bar of 3 chords is to emphasize the bass notes of the chord, so that a run is heard.*
> 2 - *When a piece finishes with 2 bars of the same chord, end the piece by playing a strong downbeat on the first beat of the last bar. This gives a good positive ending.*

5. With a rock blues beat

To Coda ⊕

D.C. al Coda

⊕ *Coda*

Tip: *Keep the chord positions as close as possible to either the 4th fret or 9th fret, but make that choice before you start.*

6. Slow & reflective

𝄞 ⁶⁄₈ Dbmaj7	%	Ebm6	Fm7
pp	*p*		

To Coda ⊕

Gbmaj7	Gb6	Absus4	Ab7
mp			

Db6	Bbm7.. Am7..	Absus4	Ab7
f			

D.C. al Coda

Gbmaj7	Ebm7	Dbmaj7	Ab7
mp			

⊕ *Coda*

Db6	Gb6	Fm7	Gb6
mf			

Ebm	Absus4	Ab7	Dbmaj7

7. With a beat

| Bb | D7 | Eb | Bbmaj7 |

f

| Bb7 | C7 | Fsus4 | F7 |

To Coda ⊕

𝄋 | Bb | D7 | Eb | Cm |

p

| Bb | F | Bb | F7 |

mf

| Ebmaj7 | Eb6 | Bbmaj7 | Bb6 |

D.S. al Coda

| Cm | Cm7 | Fsus4 | F7 |

⊕ *Coda*

| Bb | F | Bbmaj7 | Bb6 |

f

8. Fast funky tempo

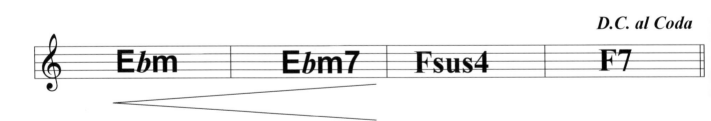

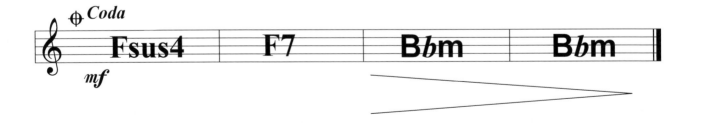

9. In a thoughtful mood

To Coda ⊕

| Cmaj7 | Am7 | Dm6 | Gsus4 |

pp

| Fmaj7 | F6 | Cmaj7 | G7 |

p

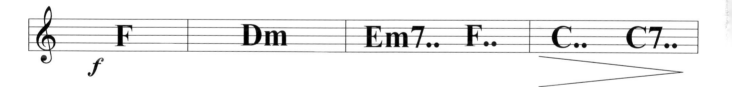

| F | Dm | Em7.. F.. | C.. C7.. |

f

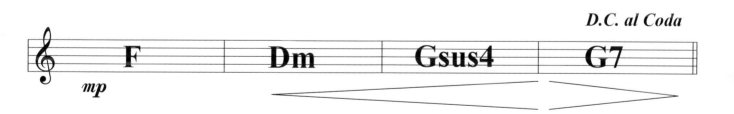

D.C. al Coda

| F | Dm | Gsus4 | G7 |

mp

⊕ *Coda*

| Cmaj7 | Dm7.. Em7.. | Fmaj7.. G7.. | Cmaj7 |

pp

10. Lively

Gm | Gm6. Gm7. | D7 | Dsus4
mf

To Coda ⊕

Cm | Cm7 | B♭6 | B♭maj7
f

E♭maj7 | D7 | B♭ | D7
mp

D.S. al Coda

Gm | Gm6. Gm7. | Cm | Dsus4. D7.
f

⊕ Coda

Cm | E♭maj7 | D7 | Gm
mp

Glossary of musical terms

Accent	....	Play louder on a particular beat.
Al Coda	....	Go to the Coda (end section)
Coda	....	A musical ending.
D.C.	....	(Da Capo = from the head) play from the beginning.
D.S.	....	(Dal Segno = from the sign) play from the sign marked 𝄋
Dynamics	....	Changes in volume.
Frets	....	Metal strips that divide up the fingerboard.
Fretbuzz	....	The buzzing sound that occurs if you don't press the strings firmly and close to the frets with the tips of your fingers.
Harmony	....	The sound of two or more notes being played together.
Plectrum	....	A triangular object (usually) made of plastic, that is used to strike the strings.
Rubato	....	('Robbed time') An artistic fluctuation of tempo within a musical phrase.
Sequence	....	A section of music usually constructed of a set number of bars.
Sim.	....	Keep playing in a similar fashion.
Split-bar	....	Where two or more chords occur in a single bar.
Syncopation	....	Featuring the 'off-beat' as the main accented part.
Tempo	....	Overall speed.
Time signature	....	The numbers which occur at the beginning of all written music that inform you of the number of beats per bar, and the value of each beat.

CHORD SUMMARY

The solid black line on the third fret shown in all diagrams on this page indicates that all six strings should be fretted, using the first finger as a barre.

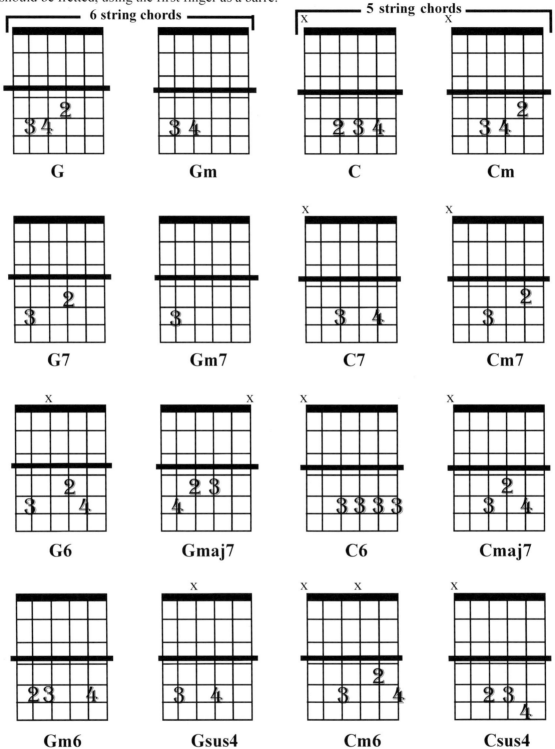

All of the chords above have been shown as G for the 6 string shapes and C for the 5 string shapes, but all of them can be played on any fret using the chart below.

For a sharp move one fret higher and for a flat move one fret lower. For example, D*b* would be on the 9th fret as a 6 string shape and on the 4th fret as a 5 string shape.

frets	1	2	3	4	5	6	7	8	9	10	11	12
6 string	F		G		A		B	C		D		E
5 string		B	C		D		E	F		G		A